# better off

## Griselda Meek

BookLeaf Publishing
India | USA | UK

Presentation by *BookLeaf Publishing*

Web: www.bookleafpub.com

E-mail: info@bookleafpub.com

ISBN: 9789360943288

First edition 2024

*to who encouraged me that my words are
not dead or gone, unless I let my mouth stay
shut*

# PREFACE

my life is a miracle. maybe that seems a bit dramatic, but honestly, that's just embracing who I am. I am not who I thought I would be. the woman I imagined at five, ten, fifteen years old is not the woman I see in the mirror. each of those girls imagined I was someone else. I'm so grateful to be this woman though, of all of them. I am beautiful, and smart, and I am full of hope and love to give. I was made to love, and to be loved, and smile at least once every day, for my sanity. I was once someone entirely different, a girl I love so much more now than when I was her, and that brings me hope. because I will love this self when I'm 30. so why should I wait until I'm 30?

I am rainbows! sunshine! a light breeze! a splash of rain! I'm a budding flower! a light in the dark! a warmth someone needs!

# pomegranate

I'm so messy and hard to get into
peeling through me piece by piece
delicately as you can
patiently as you can
you might never get all of me
I so easily spill onto the floor
and I'm such a chore to taste
but if you took the time
if you cared enough
if you caught every seed
I'm mouth-watering
delectable
you lick the juice off your thumbs
savoring every drop
I will stain your teeth and fingers
and you'll never be rid of me

# think it was supposed to taste like starfruit

I drink from the soda can you left in my car last
night
allowing my lips to brace where yours were
a kiss from me to you
without the blessing of lips
the fondness of you in my heart
you were sad I couldn't taste it because the gum
in my mouth was minty
I sip from the flat can without you here
indulging in what I imagined the taste was
I imagine it was wonderful yesterday
but the day after it's never as good as it was

# falling

I can feel myself
beginning my descent
walking down this winding staircase
beginning to fall
I can feel myself
tripping over my words
swooning for yours
biting my tongue
I can feel myself
turning red
putting on my rose glasses
tasting a new color palette
I can feel myself
in your chest
slowly creeping into your heart
finding my way to your soul
I can feel myself
falling
definitely falling

# more than

I imagine the ability to put my thoughts into words. the knowledge of how to collect these strings of screaming fragments and connect them together. for me to be able to preach more than LOVE and LOVE and LOVE. I wish desperately to express the quantity (infinite), the depth (infinite). I wish I had more than infinite. I wish I had the ability to explain the seas of Neptune, the vastness of them, the density. I wish I could describe the softest pinks and deepness of purples and warmth of oranges and how that connects to you. I wish I could explain to you how the moon is so bright I can feel it bursting in my chest. I wish I could pinpoint how the stars sparkling speaks of you, how the softness of bed feels like you. I imagine the ability to express how you feel like giggling, like childhood and wonder, like tripping and falling and being helped up and laughing and running without missing a beat. I wish I could tell you how much I love you, that my heart could speak more than gibberish, I wish I could tell you how I felt.

# new kind of love?

he loves all the things
you hated about me
he wants to dance
he wants to keep our memories
in pictures and in words
he wants to hold me
he wants to kiss me when I laugh
he envelopes me when I won't
he adores my family
and loves my body
he understands me
more than you ever tried to
he'd never lay a finger on me
or ever want to make me cry
he only wants what's best for me
and what will make me smile
and the biggest difference
between you
and him
is that he loves me
more than you ever wanted to

# infatuated

"puppy love isn't healthy"
"spending this much time with someone isn't
good"
but we like to spend that time together
he always says he loves me
"I haven't seen you in months"
"you're doing it again"
I'll see you soon I promise
"I think he's bad for you"
"I don't like you with him"
but he's been nothing but good to me
he's done nothing that bad
what's wrong?
where's the red?

# it starts

I can see shifts in myself
the way I move less
talk less
see less
I can feel myself disappearing
drowning in you
beginning to suffocate
I let you take a nibble of me
a bite
a chunk
I'm beginning to fade away
to become unseen
I'm covered in clumps of you
your guts
your soul
and mine…
mine is…

# drowning

one bad day
and then the next bad day
today
and tomorrow
and tomorrow
every morning refusing to stretch
refusing to smile
slowly diminishing that will I gathered
batting away my reasons to be happy
shushing my laughter
holding my breath
are you… smothering my soul?

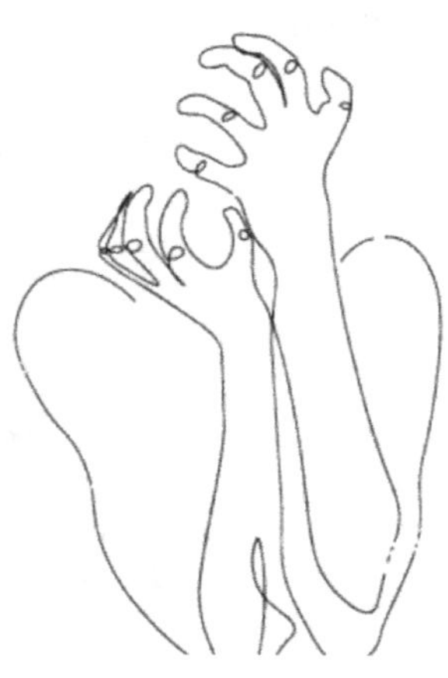

# the ick

today, I encountered the devil
around her, I felt nothing
only giggles trembled out of my throat
tonight, I went to the man who told me she was
the devil
and he made me cry
is she the devil?
or did the devil drive her to insanity?

# men have said

"you look so pretty when you cry
you should see how your eyes sparkle"
"can you tone it down a little
you're so obnoxious"
"are you seriously eating right now?
haven't you had enough?"
"I like spending time with you
but not that often"
"be careful
she has birthing hips"
"no one cares about your niche interests
stop bringing them up"
"you're embarrassing me
tone it down"
I have said
nothing

# locking my journal

I am never giving someone my poetry again.
It makes the monster grow.
I see my love ignite something inside men and
fan flames that I am too afraid of.
I didn't mean it like that.
their ego eats my words until it towers over me.
a big, looming, scary monster man.
I didn't mean it like that.

# no drawbridge

I am an empire and a fortress. My walls are so
thick, so tall, so vastly large there seems to be no
beginning or end.
I have a trap door, safely and discreetly installed
miles down the way. Somehow, you found it.
You crawled through my catacombs and trekked
your way through my elaborate maze, dodging
every sabotage I threw in the path before you.
You found the way into my palace, and onwards
to my hearth.
You sat, listening to the walls groan and weep,
warming your hands on the barely lit fire. You,
ever so skillfully, balanced new logs across my
coals. You waited with a patience no one had yet
attempted and sat quietly watching the small
flame gently lick the wood as if it were testing
for poison. After a moment or two, the flames
cackled and roared, indulging in a fresh treat.
You added another as she began to stabilize. You
continued to sit, to watch, and smile as you
warmed your hands against her. The crackling
wood drowned out the cries of the walls, warmth

filling the room around you. When you went to
add more, you realized you had used the last log.
As the fire began to die, you stood up and
abandoned the castle, as it had no more use.
You abandoned me.

# Venus fly trap

you told me you wanted an Addams family
greenhouse
carnivorous plants lining the walls
growing from the floorboards
pitcher plants hanging by windows
sundew cracking through tiles
a corpse flower only blooming once every dozen
years
and only for a day
you'd tell me to try her fruit
you'd probably beg me to choke

# again

you manipulated me
in an impressive manner
it's happened to me before
many times
should I be impressed?
with your ability to make me feel?
like nothing?
should I be impressed?
with my stupidity for letting this happen?
again?
should I be ashamed?
of myself?
for always falling for the same line?
or should you be ashamed?
for choosing such an easy target?
one that already has lines rehearsed
one that already knows commands
one that already knows her place?

# misery loves company

you're a deep pit
an endless, beautiful chasm
I was mesmerized by your beauty
and ignored the darkness underneath
I pretended I couldn't hear
the screams of the damned
the endless echoes stretching across the hollow
mass
I ventured in
and swallowed the fear in my gut
I ignored the signs to go back
turn around
before it's too late
I crawled deep inside of you
finding a cold, damp cave
I convinced myself I could keep a fire
tried to blow breath into dying embers
failing, gasping,
convincing myself I was cozy

# pretty words are deadly

I fall for the things you say
the promises and deep glances
understanding we can't
go on dates
be together in public
you can't be seen with me
but we're so in love
you call me late at night
drunk
alone
singing words of love
preaching promises you've yet to keep
endless words you've yet to prove
but I love you
so I believe you
and this endless web of lies

# fault

at what point is it my fault?
the first time
when I didn't quite say no
I didn't say anything
freezing
silent tears slipping away into my laundry
the second time
when I struggled under his weight
suffocating
not pushing back hard enough
the third time
when I blacked out
and came to on top of him
the fourth time
when I finally DID say no
over and over
and over
and he didn't believe me
take me seriously
when it happens this much
isn't it my fault?

# you make me sick

I have another cold sore and I'm thinking of you.
while I've had them my whole life,
I only get them when I'm sick or stressed.
previous years I've had one, maybe two
the past few months I've had half a dozen.
I haven't gotten sick,
and most else of my life is golden.
it's just you

# the carpet

I'm melting away
pooling underneath
slipping through the cloth
I'm spilled across the floor
staining the carpet
the floorboards
I am etched into this house
I've been here for so long
leaving feels so
wrong

# thinking of the past

she's wearing my shirt.
it looks better on her than it ever did me.
"you can keep it," I say.
"no, it's yours," she says.
she gives it back to me after we leave.
it smells like her.
I'm too afraid to wash it.
I don't want the trace of her gone.
we used to share a closet.
her clothes and my clothes mixed together.
her pants are my pants.
my shirts are hers.
I loved the chaos, the messy room, the unmade
bed.
she was a tornado in my life,
but she made it more exciting.

# in and out

we fall out of love for the reason we fell in
I used to adore your stubbornness
your unwillingness to change
your foot on the ground for what is right by you
the stubbornness
your unwillingness to change
is the very reason
we can't even speak

# the net

I have always prided myself in being a safe
space
I found solace in knowing I'd always be here
for you
(I'll always be here for anybody)
my shoulders are chipping and I am eroding
I am simply crumbling apart
the helping hand has broken off
and my ears can't seem to listen
what am I if not here for you?
what am I if I am not ignoring myself?
my own needs?
my wants?
if I can't be a safe space for you
what am I supposed to be?
a safe place for myself?
I had never thought of that

# tear burn

I took a shower this morning
hoping it would make pools of my empty
catacombs
hoping the second-degree burns would make my
back stand tall
begging to melt the skin off my bones
begging for my tissue down the drain
it just fanned my anger
making me hotter
the water refuses to douse the flame

# dry well

I can't rot in your home anymore
I've poured all of myself into your hands
just to spill from your fingers
I have no water left for my own garden
because I used it all on yours
you finally start to bloom and show color
I, exhausted, walk home to check on mine
heartbroken, I see my flowers have wilted
gophers have eaten all my strawberries
and the fairies are nowhere to be seen
I go to weep, but I'm dry, my tears can't come
with my head low, I walk inside
my cat doesn't greet me
he bites me, claws up my legs
it's not his fault, he too is left begging for my
love
when I have none left

# thank you.

for opening me up,
for dissecting me.
for finding every little thing about me
that you thought was wrong.
for chewing me into little tiny pieces.
for leaving me in smaller shards than you found.
for stepping on me.
crushing me.

I thought leaving you would be so freeing.

# to bleed

I just want to take a bite out of the sky
savor the stars and feel them on my tongue
I want my mouth to bleed
covered in the galaxy
I just want pine needles to fill my mouth
and get stuck between my teeth
I want my mouth to bleed
sap pouring from my lips
I just want to devour rocks
to feel the grain clatter with my teeth
I want my mouth to bleed
dirt leaving with my breath
I just want to be connected
to something
I want my mouth to bleed

# won't

I can't make you see anything
my eyes are not your eyes
my life is not yours
I can't explain the experiences I've had
the challenges I've faced
the monsters I've dueled
my warnings you pay no mind to
the words you do not heed
I can't make you do anything you don't want to
I can't hold your hand through every bad fight
I can scream all I want
put stop signs
yield signs
wherever I please
it's not my job
my fault
to make you do what you don't want to

# my girl

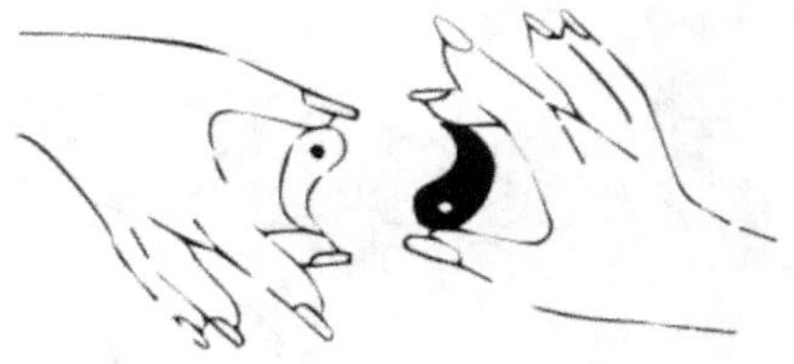

I forever prefer the time with her
late giggling into the night
soft and innocent and wholesome
holding each other when we cry
licking our wounds together
bandaging eachother up
friendships that heal your soul
huddled together during breakfast
diving into the things that make us us
I will always crave
being held by friends
never draining my energy
never taking
never feeling like I'm being poured out
only tender love
undying devotion
unwavering support
the kind of unconditional
I could never get from somewhere else

# too enough

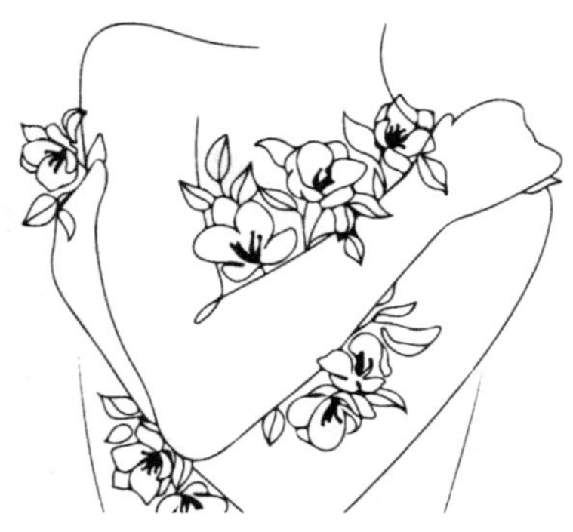

my whole life I've been told I'm
not pretty enough
not skinny enough
not enough
my whole life I've been told I'm
much too loud
much too sensitive
much too much
my whole life I was never
good enough
for anyone
the only words I'm hearing now
the only ones I'll pay attention to
are "too"
and "enough"
I will not be sorry
for being too enough for you

# a perfect blend

I strive to be a peaceful presence
I was put on earth to make you feel at ease
I carry my mother's sorrow
my father's timidness
his silence
her wailing
I inherited years of weight
of unsaid words
of unkept promises
I wear my mother's smile
the bags under her eyes
I wear my father's hands
the wrinkle between his brows
I sing my mother's laugh
my dad's dry jokes
my mother's resilience
my father's composure
I am both
as different as they are
as different as I am
as I can be
I am both

# March

I live for this spring cleaning
to watch the dead come back to life
for flowers to bloom
to open the windows
feeling the kiss of wind through the glass
the quiet hum of life outside
to blow the dust off
the clean home healing my insides
this feels like a rebirth
Persephone has come back from the underworld
it's much brighter now
more hopeful
I left him behind
leaving Hades in hell
right where he belongs

# how to write

my words aren't perfect
I'm not
this mass sea of words
my incoherent string of thought
do I make any sense?
to anyone?
myself?
the poems in me are itching
I don't know how to get them out
I'm clawing and clawing
I choke on words stuck in my throat
nothing makes sense
nothing has cadence
nothing rhymes
what am I doing wrong?

# reconnect

I'm falling back in love with nature
I stare outside my window for hours
I drive home at night staring at the stars
I lie in bed at night holding myself
I fall asleep to my own breath
I wake up stretched like a starfish
I absorb the sun in my hands
I let the rays beat into my face
I'm becoming whole again
I am becoming whole again

# are you absorbing?

putting myself out like this
feels like bleeding out
like drowning in the bath
I'm trembling as I write
I can't fathom the idea of sharing
I'm being too much
too much
I feel naked
bare
what are you thinking
reading my innermost thoughts
what are you thinking?

# muddy

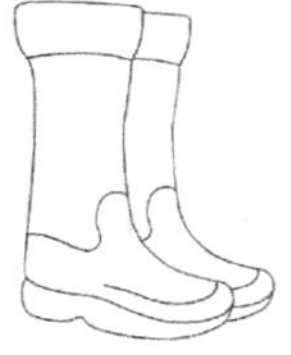

I'm standing in a puddle
a borderline lake in my mind
the way it's taken over the huge pit in my
backyard
it goes up near the top of my rainboots
the wind creates ripples
I feel myself sinking slowly
I absorb the trees
the bug sounds
the leaves trembling softly
I sink a little more
feel the water shifting over my feet
the mud crawling up my ankles
the water threatening to creep over the top
I close my eyes
and I breathe
and I'm thinking
this is life?
this is peace?

# yesterday's me

she's trembling
fingers too afraid to press a key
thoughts running faster than I ever really could
heart pumping
heart shaking
what if no one buys it?
what if no one likes it?
what if no one cares?
she's hesitating
shaking
shivering
the thoughts are running
just put them down
just put them down
I press a key

# sooner

the sooner I begin to write again
and the color sprouts from my fingertips
and sonnets pour from my mouth
the sooner I see color
and the stars in my eyes are back
the sooner I begin to move
and from my bones and aching muscles grow
flowers
the sooner I begin to breathe
and my tired lungs fill with air
and I fill myself with unadulterated motives
the sooner I remove myself
and I finally begin to unstick
and peel
from my terrible habits and tormented thoughts
the sooner I begin to live
and smile and laugh and dance
the sooner I begin to be happy again

# good morning

I am bubbly in the morning
a gentle shake will make me explode
I'm violent when I wake
well, usually
other mornings
more so lately
I wake up easy and bright
my hands stretching to the sky
my fingers separated
excited to be awake
excited to be alive

sometimes I look at pictures of myself when I
was young
when I was 7 I was adorable
admiring my big smile
when I was 13 I was so cute
adoring how awkward I was
when I was 17 I was so pretty
the way I wish I looked now
someday I will be 30
reflecting on images of myself now
and I will smile
and say I was so beautiful
so beautiful
why am I waiting until I'm 30?

# better off

every day is a project
every day is a step
every day is a breath
everything I do
is something I'm afraid of
I'm still scared
I'm still thirteen
I'm still shy
still unsure
but every day is a project
a step
a breath
something I was once too afraid to do
I'm doing better
good even
I'm proud of myself
and every fall I took

# zelda

I imagine a me more powerful
formidable and passionate
the girl who has finally found herself
in platform boots and sundresses
in sticker bombs and spray paint
in screaming and breaking glass
in putting her foot down
in saying no
in letting be
I imagine myself at fifteen
shaking in my converse
I see myself standing over her
holding her cheeks and knowing what she
doesn't
in knowing it will be alright
in I will always be okay
in my platform boots
and the dresses I was too afraid to wear

# …pomegranate

I hope I stained your fingers
I hope I'm stuck in your teeth
I hope I linger on your tongue
I hope you have to carry me everywhere you go

www.ingramcontent.com/pod-product-compliance
Lightning Source LLC
Chambersburg PA
CBHW061725130726
47996CB00006B/2511